# THE 'KEY' OF JACOB BOEHME

JACOB BEHMEN

THE TEVTONIC THEOSOPHER BORN AT OLD SEIDENBVRG 1575 DIED AT GORLITZ 1624

Hark! What that Angel sounds, whom Jesus chose,
In Time most fit for his Mysteries to disclose.
See! Wisdom Light Humility adorn;
Of good the Loves of evil Men the Scorn.

# THE 'KEY' OF JACOB BOEHME

WITH

## AN ILLUSTRATION OF THE DEEP PRINCIPLES OF JACOB BEHMEN

by D. A. Freher

TRANSLATED BY
WILLIAM LAW

WITH AN INTRODUCTORY ESSAY
BY ADAM MCLEAN

MAGNUM OPUS HERMETIC SOURCEWORKS #9

PHANES PRESS
1991

This work, part of the Magnum Opus Hermetic Sourceworks series, was previously published in a handbound edition, limited to 250 copies, in 1981. The Magnum Opus Hermetic Sourceworks series is published under the General Editorship of Adam McLean.

Introduction © 1991 by Adam McLean

98 97 96 95 94 93 92 91   5 4 3 2 1

Published by Phanes Press, PO Box 6114, Grand Rapids, MI 49516, USA.

**Library of Congress Cataloging-in-Publication Data**

Böhme, Jakob, 1575-1624.
    [Clavis. English]
    The 'Key' of Jacob Boehme / translated by William Law ; with an introductory essay by Adam McLean. With an illustration of the deep principles of Jacob Behmen / by Dionysius Andrew Freher.
       p.   cm.
    Translation of: Clavis.
    ISBN 0-933999-93-3 (alk. paper) — ISBN 0-933999-94-1 (pbk. : alk. paper)
    1. Mysticism—Germany. 2. Böhme, Jakob, 1575-1624. 3. Mysticism—Germany—History—16th century. 4. Mysticism—Germany—History—17th century. 5. Mysticism—Lutheran Church. 6. Lutheran Church—Doctrines—History—16th century. 7. Lutheran Church—Doctrines—History—17th century. I. McLean, Adam. II. Freher, D. A., 1649-1728. Illustration of the deep principles of Jacob Behmen. 1991. III. Title. IV. Series: Magnum Opus Hermetic Sourceworks (Series) ; no. 9.
    BV5095.B7B5813 1991
    248.2'2—dc20                  90-47418
                                        CIP

This book is printed on alkaline paper which conforms to the permanent paper standard developed by the National Information Standards Organization.

Printed and bound in the United States

# Contents

# Introduction

Jacob Boehme (1575–1624), 'The German Theosopher' whose creative life spanned the Rosicrucian period, was a mystic whose insights did much to establish a spiritual interpretation of alchemy. Although an unscholared shoemaker, Boehme had a high degree of mystical perception of the spiritual worlds, and chose when expressing his inner experiences to clothe them in alchemical terms. He had a profound influence on esoteric and theological ideas, particularly during the late seventeenth and early eighteenth centuries, though his esoteric-philosophical system of theology continues to inspire people to this day.

Boehme came from a relatively humble family background. He was born in 1675 in the village of Old Seidenburg and was brought up in Upper Lusatia on the borders of Bohemia during the closing decades of the sixteenth century. He was apprenticed to a shoemaker and was later to establish himself as a prosperous citizen in the nearby town of Gorlitz.

When he was a young apprentice shoemaker working in his master's shop, Boehme met with a mysterious stranger who had a profound impact upon his life. Manly Palmer Hall tells the story in this way:

> One day while tending his master's shoe shop, a mysterious stranger entered who, while he seemed to possess but little of this world's goods, appeared to be most wise and noble in spiritual attainment. The stranger asked the price of a pair of shoes, but young Boehme did not dare to name a figure, for fear that he would displease his master. The stanger insisted and Boehme finally placed a valuation which he felt was all that his master possibly could hope to secure for the shoes. The stranger immediately bought them and departed. A short distance down the street the mysterious stranger stopped and cried out in a loud voice, "Jakob, Jakob, come forth." In amazement and fright, Boehme ran out of the house. The strange man fixed his eyes upon the youth—great eyes which sparkled and seemed filled with divine light. He took

the boy's right hand and addressed him as follows: "Jakob, thou art little, but shalt be great, and become another man, such a one as at whom the World shall wonder. Therefore be pious, fear God and reverence His Word. Read diligently the Holy Scriptures, wherein you shall have comfort and instruction. For thou must endure much misery and poverty, and suffer persecution, but be courageous and persevere, for God loves and is gracious to thee." Deeply impressed by the prediction, Boehme became even more intense in his search for the truth. At last his labors were rewarded. For seven days he remained in a mysterious condition during which time the mysteries of the invisible world were revealed to him.

Boehme described his visionary experience as follows:

> I saw the Being of all Beings, the Ground and the Abyss; also the birth of the Holy Trinity; the origin and the first state of the world and of all creatures. I saw in myself the three worlds—the Divine or angelic world; the dark world, the original of Nature; and the external world, as a substance spoken forth out of the two spiritual worlds . . . In my inward man I saw it well, as in a great deep; for I saw right through as into a chaos where everything lay wrapped, but I could not unfold it. Yet from time to time it opened itself within me like a growing plant. For twelve years I carried it about within me, before I could bring it forth in any external form; till afterwards it fell upon me, like a bursting shower that kills where it lands, as it will. Whatever I could bring into outwardness I wrote down. The work is none of mine; I am but the Lord's instrument, with which He does what He wills.

Boehme's life was greatly shaped by two Lutheran Pastors at Gorlitz. The first, Martin Möller, was a remarkable man of broad learning and mystical leanings, who organized within his parish a small group, 'The Conventicle of God's Real Servants,' which had Boehme as a member. This seems to have been some kind of mystical meditative group working in the spirit of the Christian mystical tradition, and Möller, through his strong personality, was able to continue this within the sphere of Lutheran orthodoxy. Under his tutelage, Boehme gained confidence in his own spiritual perceptions and in time began to write, initially merely for his own edification, his first volume, *The Aurora*, which he completed in 1612. Copies of this were circulated without Boehme's permission, and outraged the new Pastor of Gorlitz, Gregory Richter, who had by then replaced Möller. Richter was of a totally opposite disposition to Möller, being narrow and orthodox, and frightened of anything that did not conform to Lutheran teachings. He denounced Boehme as a heretic and stirred up such a current of opposition in the parish that Boehme was temporarily banished from the city. Boehme had to promise to cease from writing, and indeed, for the next seven years, he worked only inwardly with his perceptions. However, he later came into a circle of Paracelsian alchemists, the most prominent member being Balthasar Walter, who was widely travelled, having even visited Greece, Syria, and Egypt. Walter, who was physician to the Prince of Anhalt, had many contacts among important people and it is likely that he was actively involved in the Rosicrucian movement. He constantly encouraged Boehme to write, and inspired him by introducing him to ideas from the esoteric traditions of alchemy and Kabbalah, which mirrored Boehme's inner experiences, and enabled him to create a language in which to fashion these. From 1619 until his death, Boehme worked to write his vast volumes:

*The Three Principles of the Divine Essence*
*The Signature of All Things*
*Mysterium Magnum*
*Concerning the Election of Grace*
*Forty Questions Concerning the Soul*
*The Way to Christ*
*The Threefold Life of Man*

Also during this period, Boehme corresponded with contacts made through Balthasar Walter, and his reputation spread through these letters. Some of his writings were privately circulated amongst his friends, but their publication had to await Boehme's death as

Pastor Richter still saw Boehme as a dangerous heretic in his parish, and Boehme's highly-placed friends could not guard him from the fanaticism of this pastor.

Boehme's writings were, after his death in 1624, quickly published and also translated into Dutch. English editions were issued by John Sparrow in the 1650s. Boehme's occult-philosophical ideas thus began to have an influence upon British mystics of the late seventeenth century, particularly John Pordage (1607–1681), and Jane Leade (1620–1704), who was to establish the Boehmist influenced 'Philadelphian Society' in the last decade of the seventeenth century. This movement for religious renewal through inner mystical experience drew into its small fold some influential and dedicated souls: Richard Roach, Francis Lee and others; although the center focus of its inspiration lay in the strong mystical personality of Jane Leade, who it might be fair to describe as the 'English Boehme.' Certainly her work was not as vast as Boehme's, nor her abilities at communicating her insights so broad, but she did share with him a direct mystical communion with the spiritual world.

At almost the same time, there was a small group of Boehmists in Germany centered around George Gichtel (1638–1710), who was editing Boehme's works and illustrating them with emblematic figures. One of Gichtel's followers, Dionysius Andreas Freher (1647–1725), settled in England, attracted by the fame of Jane Leade and the Philadelphian Society. Freher gathered around him his own group of followers and worked to fashion his own interpretation of Boehme's philosophy.

Thus Boehmist philosophy was perpetuated as a living stream nourished by this string of personalities: Gichtel, Pordage, Leade, and Freher, who each in their own way possessed some share of mystical insight. They used Boehme's philosophy as a means of focussing their mystic perception and making it communicable to others, for Boehme incarnated a system of ideas which enabled people to describe and clothe mystical experiences. Perhaps, in this, lies his greatest achievement.

The influence of Boehme continued into the middle of the eighteenth century through the figure of the Reverend William

Law (1686–1761). Early in his life Law was attracted by the writings of Jacob Boehme, and indeed had his own mystical leanings. He became quite well-known as a non-establishment theologian and this led the young John Wesley (who was later to found Methodism) at one point to seek Law's advice. Later in his life, Law set about translating and editing the entire body of Boehme's writings for publication in English. This vast four-volume set, *The Works of Jacob Behmen, The Teutonic Theosopher*, was published in 1764, and is the best-known of all English editions of Boehme. Through this publication Boehme's mystical philosophy continued to influence various British writers, and in particular, William Blake. Blake's vast systems of archetypal beings emanating in polarities mirrors Boehme's own picturing of a process of Thesis-Antithesis-Synthesis occuring even on the highest spiritual level.

Finally, we can trace Boehme's thoughts in the early codification of the Theosophical Society founded by Madame Blavatsky in the closing decades of the nineteenth century, and thus his occult-mystical philosophy permeated through and tinctured the mainstream of twentieth-century esotericism. Thus we find that Boehme's philosophy is still alive today, worked into the formative ideas and thought forms of present-day esotericism. His writings are an important source we can dip into for new inspirations and insights into the archetypal forms of familiar esoteric ideas.

With Boehme, an important turning point in the evolution of Western Esotericism is reached, as he indirectly contributed to widening the gap between the purely physical operation of alchemy and the pursuit of alchemy as a spiritual-philosophical system. This gulf which existed in germ at the beginning of the seventeenth century widened until a purely materialistic chemistry was born in the eighteenth century. Boehme, however, drew upon both inner mystical experiences and the practical experiences of the alchemists of that time (we should remember that through Balthasar Walter he was actively involved in a circle of practicing Paracelsian alchemists); if we are sensitive to this, we can see in his writings both ways of uniting praxis and theoria, as well as ways of separating them into two distinct realms. Boehme thus worked to incarnate a Soul Alchemy, and his writings are profound documents of a

Protestant esotericism which places the burden of inner develop-
ment squarely upon the soul of the individual. In this Protestant
esotericism, it is the task of the individual to work to purify and
exalt his own soul forces, if he is to achieve the end of the work.

Boehme's writings are of great length and unfold a vast system
of ideas, a web of spiritual thoughts, which arose not out of arid
intellectualization, but out of his own living communion with the
spiritual world. In his volumes he reveals an esoteric Christianity
which surely bears some direct connection with the esoteric
stream of Rosicrucianism that was being unfolded contemporarily
with Boehme.

He was aware of the difficulty of his books and consequently
wrote the *Clavis* or 'Key' to his writings, as a summary of the main
ideas in his system. Here he deals with the existence of polarities,
the Thesis-Antithesis-Synthesis, which lies at the foundation of a
Hermetic-alchemical view of the world; the Three Principles, Salt,
Mercury and Sulphur, and their manifestation as archetypes in
various realms; and the Seven Properties, which connect with the
Planetary archetypes, which also bear within them polarity and the
three principles. *The Key of Jacob Boehme* provides us with an easy
introduction to the main points of his philosophy and should make
it easier for us to approach his larger works.

Appended to this in the William Law edition is Dionysius
Freher's *Illustration of the Deep Principles of Jacob Behmen*, which,
through a series of thirteen emblematic figures, unfolds the Boehmist
picture of Creation. Here we see the various emanations of the
Godhead participating in the formation of the Earth realm. This
further unfolds a picture of a Cosmic Christianity, showing the
descent of the Christ Being into the human sphere and the fulfill-
ment of His task there.

I trust that by bringing these two short works to the attention
of students of esotericism today, I may have enabled them to
approach nearer to an understanding of the vast system of esoteric
philosophy that poured through the mystical insight of Jacob
Boehme.

—ADAM MCLEAN

# THE

# C L A V I S:

## O R

An EXPLANATION of some principal POINTS and
EXPRESSIONS in his WRITINGS.

By JACOB BEHMEN, the Teutonic Theosopher.

# THE

# AUTHOR's PREFACE

*It is written,* the Natural Man receives not the Things of the Spirit, nor the Mystery of the Kingdom of God, they are Foolishness unto him, neither can he know them: *therefore I admonish and exhort the Christian Lover of Mysteries, if he will study these High Writings, and read, search, and understand them, that he does not read them outwardly only, with sharp Speculation and Meditation; for in so doing, he shall remain in the outward Imaginary Ground only, and obtain no more than a counterfeited Colour of them.*

*For a Man's own Reason, without the Light of God, cannot come into the Ground [of them], it is impossible; let his Wit be ever so high and subtle, it apprehends but as it were the Shadow of it in a Glass.*

*For Christ says,* without me you can do nothing; *and he is the Light of the World, and the Life of Men.*

*Now if any one would search the Divine Ground, that is, the Divine Revelation, he must first consider with himself, for what End he desires to know such Things; whether he desires to practice that which he might obtain, and bestow it to the Glory of God and the Welfare of his Neighbour; and whether he desires to die to Earthliness, and to his own Will, and to live in that which he seeks and desires, and to be one Spirit with it.*

*If he has not a Purpose, that if God should reveal himself and his Mysteries to him, he would be one Spirit and have one Will with him, and wholly resign himself up to him, that God's Spirit might do what he pleases with him, and by him, and that God*

15

might be his Knowledge, Will, and Deed, he is not yet fit for such Knowledge and Understanding.

For there are many that seek Mysteries and hidden Knowledge, merely that they might be respected and highly esteemed by the World, and for their own Gain and Profit; but they attain not this Ground, where the Spirit searches all Things, as it is written, even the deep Things of God.

It must be a totally resigned Will, in which God himself searches and works, and which continually pierces into God in yielding and resigned Humility, seeking nothing but his Eternal Native Country, and to do his Neighbour Service with it, and then it may be attained; and he must begin with effectual Repentance and Amendment, and with Prayer, that his Understanding might be opened from within; for then the inward will bring itself into the outward.

But when he reads such Writings, and yet cannot understand them, he must not presently throw them away, and think it is impossible to understand them; no, but he must turn his Mind to God, beseeching him for Grace and Understanding, and read again, and then he shall see more and more in them, till at length he is drawn by the Power of God into the very Depth itself, and so comes into the supernatural and supersensual Ground, namely into the Eternal Unity of God; where he shall hear unspeakable and effectual Words of God, which shall bring him back and outward again, by the Divine Effluence, to the very grossest and meanest Matter of the Earth, and back and inwards to God again; then the Spirit of God searches all Things with him, and by him, and so he is rightly taught and driven by God.

But since the Lovers of them desire a Clavis, or Key of my Writings, I am ready and willing to pleasure them in it, and will set down a short Description of the Ground of those unusual Words; some of which are taken from Nature and Sense, and some are the Words of uncommon Masters, which I have tried according to

*Sense, and found them good and fit.*

*Reason will stumble, when it sees Heathenish Terms and Words used in the Explanation of Natural Things, supposing we should use none but Scripture Phrase (or words borrowed from the Bible); but such Words will not always apply and square themselves to the fundamental Explanation of the Properties of Nature, neither can a Man express the Ground with them: Also the wise Heathens and Jews have hid the deep Ground of Nature under such Words, as having well understood that the Knowledge of Nature is not for every one, but it belongs to those only, whom God by Nature has chosen for it.*

*But none need stumble at it; for when God reveals his Mysteries to any Man, he then also brings him into a Mind and Capacity how to express them, as God knows to be most necessary and profitable in every Age, for the setting the confused Tongues and Opinions upon the true Ground again: Men must not think that it comes by Chance, and is done by human Reason.*

*The Revelations of Divine Things are opened by the Inward Ground of the Spiritual World, and brought into visible Forms, just as the Creator will manifest them.*

*I will write but a short Description of the Divine Manifestation, yet as much as I can comprise in brief; and explain the unusual Words for the better Understanding of our Books, and set down here the sum of those Writings, or a Model or Epitome of them, for the Consideration and Help of Beginners: The further Explanation of it is to be found in the other Books.*

JACOB BEHMEN

# THE
# C L A V I S;

OR,

## An Explanation of some principal Points and Expressions.

### *How God is to be considered without Nature and Creature.*

*M O S E S* saith, the Lord our God is but one only God. In another place it is said; of him, through him, and in him are all things: in another, am not I he that filleth all things? and in another, through his Word are all things made, that are made; therefore we may say, that he is the Original of all things: He is the Eternal unmeasurable unity.

For example, when I think what would be in the place of this world, if the four Elements and the starry Firmament, and also Nature itself, should perish and cease to be, so that no Nature or Creature were to be found any more; I find there would remain this Eternal Unity, from which Nature and Creature have received their Original.

So likewise, when I think with myself what is many hundred thousand miles above the starry Firmament, or what is in that place where no Creature is, I find the Eternal unchangeable unity is there, which is that only good, which has nothing either before or after it, that can add any thing to it, or take any thing away from it, or from which this unity could have its Original: There is neither ground, time, nor place, but there is the only Eternal God, or that only Good, which a man cannot express.

## A further Consideration, How this one God is Three-fold.

The Holy Scripture shows us, that this only God is Threefold, namely one only threefold Essence, having three manner of workings, and yet is but one only Essence, as may be seen in the outflown Power and Virtue which is in all things, if any does but observe it: but it is especially represented to us in Fire, Light, and Air; which are three several sorts of workings, and yet but in one only ground and substance.

And as we see that Fire, Light, and Air, arise from a Candle (though the Candle is none of the three, but a cause of them), so likewise the Eternal unity is the cause and ground of the Eternal Trinity, which manifests itself from the unity, and brings forth itself, *First*, in Desire or Will; *Secondly*, Pleasure or Delight; *Thirdly*, Proceeding or Outgoing.

The Desire, or Will, is the Father; that is, the stirring, or manifestation of the unity, whereby the unity wills or desires itself.

The Pleasure, or Delight, is the Son; and is that which the Will willeth and desireth, namely his Love and Pleasure, as may be seen at the Baptism of our Lord Jesus Christ, when the Father witnessed, saying, *This is my beloved Son, in whom I am well pleased; hear ye him.*

The Delight is the compression in the will, whereby the will in the unity brings itself into a place and working, wherewith the will willeth and worketh; and it is the feeling and virtue of the will.

The Will is the Father, that is, the stirring desire; and the Delight is the Son, that is, the virtue and the working in the will, with which the will worketh; and the Holy Ghost is the proceeding will through the Delight of the virtue, that is, a Life of the will, and of the virtue and delight.

Thus there are three sorts of workings in the Eternal Unity, namely the Unity is the will and desire of itself; the Delight is the working substance of the will, and an Eternal joy of perceptibility in the will; and the Holy Ghost is the proceeding of the Power: the similitude of which may be seen in a Plant.

The *Magnet*, namely the Essential Desire of Nature, that is, the will of the Desire of Nature, compresses itself into an *Ens* or substance, to become a Plant; and in this compression of the Desire becomes feeling, that is, working; and in that working, the Power and virtue arises, wherein the Magnetical Desire of Nature, namely the outflown will of God, works in a natural way.

In this working perceptibility, the Magnetical desiring will is elevated and made joyful, and goes forth from the working Power and Virtue; and hence comes the growing and smell of the Plant: and thus we see a representation of the Trinity of God in all growing and living things.

If there was not such a desiring perceptibility, and outgoing operation of the Trinity in the Eternal unity, the unity were but an Eternal stillness, a Nothing; and there would be no Nature, nor any Colour, Shape, or Figure; likewise there would be nothing in this world; without this threefold working, there could be no world at all.

## Of the Eternal Word of God.

The Holy Scripture saith, God has made all things by his Eternal word; also it saith, That word is God, *John* 1, which we understand thus:

The word is nothing else but the out-breathing will, from the Power and Virtue; a various dividing of the Power into a multitude of Powers; a distribution and outflowing of the unity, whence knowledge arises.

For in one only Substance, wherein there is no variation or division, but is only one, there can be no knowledge; and if there were knowledge, it could know but one thing, namely itself: but if it parts itself, then the dividing will goes into multiplicity and variety; and each separation works in itself.

Yet because Unity cannot be divided and parted asunder, therefore the separation consists and remains in the outbreathing will in the unity; and the separation of the breathing gives the different variety, whereby the Eternal will, together with the Delight and Proceeding, enters into the knowledge, or understanding of infinite Forms, namely into an Eternal perceptible working

sensual knowledge of the Powers; where always in the division of
the will, in the separation, one sense or form of the will sees, feels,
tastes, smells, and hears the other; and yet it is but one sensual
working, namely the great joyous band of Love, and the most
pleasant only Eternal Being.

## *Of the Holy Name J E H O V A.*

The Ancient Rabins among the *Jews* have partly understood it;
for they have said, that this Name is the Highest, and most Holy
Name of God; by which they understand the working Deity in
Sense: and it is true, for in this working sense lies the true life of all
things in Time and Eternity, in the Ground and Abyss; and it is God
himself, namely the Divine working Perceptibility, Sensation,
Invention, Science, and Love; that is, the true understanding in the
working unity, from which the five senses of the true Life spring.

Each Letter in this Name intimates to us a peculiar virtue and
working, that is, a Form in the working Power.

## J

For **I** is the Effluence of the Eternal indivisible Unity, or the
sweet grace and fullness of the ground of the Divine Power of
becoming something.

## E

**E** is a threefold **I**, where the Trinity shuts itself up in the Unity;
for the **I** goes into **E**, and joineth **I E**, which is an outbreathing of the
Unity itself.

## H

**H** is the Word, or breathing of the Trinity of God.

## O

**O** is the Circumference, or the Son of God, through which the
**I E** and the **H**, or breathing, speaks forth from the compressed
Delight of the Power and Virtue.

# V

**V** is the joyful Effluence from the breathing, that is, the proceeding Spirit of God.

# A

**A** is that which is proceeded from the power and virtue, namely the wisdom; a Subject of the Trinity; wherein the Trinity works, and wherein the Trinity is also manifest.

This Name is nothing else but a speaking forth, or expression of the Threefold working of the Holy Trinity in the unity of God. Read further of this in the Explanation of the Table of the three Principles of the Divine Manifestation.

## Of the Divine Wisdom.

The Holy Scripture says, the wisdom is the breathing of the Divine Power, a ray and breath of the Almighty; also it says, God has made all things by his wisdom; which we understand as follows.

The Wisdom is the outflown word of the Divine Power, Virtue, Knowledge, and Holiness; a Subject and Resemblance of the infinite and unsearchable Unity; a Substance wherein the Holy Ghost works, forms, and models; I mean, he forms and models the Divine understanding in the Wisdom; for the Wisdom is the Passive, and the Spirit of God is the Active, or Life in her, as the Soul in the Body.

The Wisdom is the Great Mystery of the Divine Nature; for in her, the Powers, Colours, and Virtues are made manifest; in her is the variation of the power and virtue, namely the understanding: she is the Divine understanding, that is, the Divine vision, wherein the Unity is manifest.

She is the true Divine Chaos, wherein all things lie, namely a Divine Imagination, in which the *Ideas* of Angels and Souls have been seen from Eternity, in a Divine Type and Resemblance; yet not then as Creatures, but in resemblance, as when a man beholds his face in a Glass: therefore the Angelical and human *Idea* flowed forth from the wisdom, and was formed into an Image, as *Moses* says, God created Man in his Image, that is, he created the body, and breathed into it the breath of the Divine Effluence, of Divine Knowledge, from all the Three Principles of the Divine Manifestation.

## *Of the* Mysterium Magnum.

The *Mysterium Magnum* is a subject of the wisdom, where the breathing word, or the working willing Power of the Divine understanding, flows forth through the wisdom, wherein also the unity of God together flows out, to its manifestation.

For in the *Mysterium Magnum* the Eternal Nature arises; and two substances and wills are always understood to be in the *Mysterium Magnum*; the first substance is the unity of God, that is, the Divine Power and Virtue, the outflowing Wisdom.

The second substance is the separable will, which arises through the breathing and outspeaking word; which will has not its ground in the unity, but in the Mobility of the Effluence and breathing forth, which brings itself into one will, and into a Desire to Nature, namely into the Properties as far as Fire and Light: in the Fire, the Natural Life is understood; and in the Light, the Holy Life, that is, a manifestation of the unity, whereby the unity becomes a Love-Fire, or Light.

And in this place or working, God calleth himself a loving, merciful God, according to the sharpened fiery burning Love of the unity; and an Angry Jealous God, according to the fiery Ground, according to the Eternal Nature.

The *Mysterium Magnum* is that *Chaos*, out of which Light and Darkness, that is, the foundation of Heaven and Hell, is flown from Eternity, and made manifest; for that foundation which we now call Hell, being a Principle of itself, is the ground and cause of the Fire in the Eternal Nature; which fire, in God, is only a burning Love; and where God is not manifested in a thing, according to the unity, there is an anguishing, painful, burning fire.

This burning Fire is but a manifestation of the Life, and of the Divine Love, by which the Divine Love, namely the unity, kindles up, and sharpens itself for the fiery working of the Power of God.

This ground is called *Mysterium Magnum*, or a *Chaos*, because good and evil rise out of it, namely Light and Darkness, Life and Death, Joy and Grief, Salvation and Damnation.

For it is the ground of Souls and Angels, and of all Eternal Creatures, as well evil as good; it is a ground of Heaven and Hell, also of the visible world, and all that is therein: therein have lain all things in one only ground, as an Image lies hid in a piece of wood before the Artificer carves it out and fashions it.

Yet we cannot say that the spiritual world has had any beginning, but has been manifested from Eternity out of that *Chaos*; for the Light has shone from Eternity in the Darkness, and the Darkness has not comprehended it; as Day and Night are in one another, and are two, though in one.

I must write distinctly, as if it had a beginning, for the better consideration and apprehension of the Divine ground of the Divine Manifestation; and the better to distinguish Nature from the Deity; also for the better understanding, from whence evil and good are come, and what the Being of all Beings is.

## Of the Center of the Eternal Nature.

By the word Center, we understand the first beginning to Nature, namely the most Inward ground, wherein the self-raised will brings itself, by a reception, into something, namely into a Natural working; for Nature is but a Tool and Instrument of God, which God's Power and Virtue works with, and yet it has its own Motion, from the outflown will of God: thus the Center is the Point or Ground of the self-reception to something; from whence something comes to be, and from thence the seven Properties proceed.

## Of the Eternal Nature, and its Seven Properties.

Nature is nothing but the Properties of the Capacity and Power of receiving the own risen Desire; which Desire rises in the variation of the Breathing Word, that is, of the Breathing Power and

Virtue, wherein the Properties bring themselves into substance; and this substance is called a Natural substance, and is not God himself.

For though God dwells through and through Nature, yet Nature comprehends him but so far, as the unity of God yields itself into, and communicates itself with a Natural Substance, and makes itself substantial, namely a substance of Light, which works by itself in Nature, and pierces and penetrates Nature; or else the unity of God is incomprehensible to Nature, that is, to the desirous Receiving.

Nature rises in the outflown word of the Divine perception and knowledge; and it is a continual framing and forming of Sciences and Perception: whatsoever the Word works by the Wisdom, that Nature frames and forms into Properties: Nature is like a Carpenter, who builds a House which the mind figured and contrived before in itself; so it is here also to be understood.

Whatsoever the Eternal mind figures in the Eternal wisdom of God in the Divine Power, and brings into an *Idea*, that Nature frames into a Property.

Nature, in its first ground, consists in seven Properties; and these seven divide themselves into infinite.

## The First Property.

The First Property is the Desire which causes and makes harshness, sharpness, hardness, cold, and substance.

## The Second Property.

The Second Property is the stirring, or Attraction of the Desire; it makes stinging, breaking, and dividing of the hardness; it cuts asunder the attracted desire, and brings it into multiplicity and variety; it is a ground of the bitter pain, and also the true Root of Life; it is the *Vulcan* that strikes fire.

## The Third Property.

The Third Property is the perceptibility and feeling in the breaking of the harsh hardness; and it is the ground of Anguish, and of the Natural will, wherein the Eternal will desires to be manifested; that is, it will be a Fire or Light, namely a flash, or shining, wherein the powers, colours, and virtues of the wisdom may appear: in these three first Properties consists the Foundation of Anger, and of Hell, and of all that is wrathful.

## The Fourth Property.

The Fourth Property is the Fire, in which the Unity appears, and is seen in the Light, that is, in a burning Love; and the wrath in the Essence of Fire.

## The Fifth Property.

The Fifth Property is the Light, with its Virtue of Love, in and with which the Unity works in a Natural substance.

## The Sixth Property.

The Sixth Property is the sound, voice, or Natural understanding, wherein the five senses work spiritually, that is, in an understanding Natural Life.

## The Seventh Property.

The Seventh Property is the Subject, or the Contents of the other Six Properties, in which they work, as the Life does in the Flesh; and this Seventh Property is rightly and truly called the Ground or Place of Nature, wherein the Properties stand in one only Ground.

## The First *S U B S T A N C E* in the Seven Properties.

We must always understand two Substances in the Seven Properties: we understand the first, according to the Abyss of these Properties, to be the Divine Being; that is, the Divine will with the outflowing Unity of God, which together flows forth through Nature, and bringeth itself into the Receiving to sharpness, that the Eternal Love may become working and sensible thereby, and that it may have something which is passive, wherein it may manifest itself, and be known, and of which also it might be desired and beloved again, namely the Aching passive Nature, which in the Love is changed into an Eternal Joyfulness: and when the Love in the Fire manifests itself in the Light, then it inflameth Nature, as the Sun a Plant, and the Fire Iron.

## The Second *S U B S T A N C E.*

The Second Substance is Nature's own Substance, which is Aching and Passive, and is the Tool and Instrument of the Agent; for where no Passiveness is, there is also no desire of Deliverance, or of something better; and where there is no desire of something better, there a thing rests within itself.

And therefore the Eternal unity brings itself by its Effluence and Separation into Nature, that it may have an object, in which it may manifest itself, and that it may love something, and be again beloved by something, that so there may be a perception, or sensible working and will.

# ☊⊙♃☋

# *An Explanation of the Seven Properties of Nature.*

## ♄ *The First Property.*

T H E First Property is a Desiring, like that of a Magnet, namely the Compression of the will; the will desires to be something, and yet it has nothing of which it may make something to itself; and therefore it brings itself into a Reception of itself, and compresses itself to something; and that something is nothing but a Magnetical Hunger, a harshness, like a hardness, whence even hardness, cold, and substance arise.

This compression or attraction overshadows itself, and makes itself a Darkness, which is indeed the Ground of the eternal and temporary Darkness: At the beginning of the world, salt, stones, and bones, and all such things were produced by this sharpness.

## ☿ *The Second Property.*

The Second Property of the Eternal Nature arises from the First, and it is the drawing or motion in the sharpness; for the Magnet makes hardness, but the motion breaketh the hardness again, and is a continual strife in itself.

For that which the Desire compresses and makes to be something, the motion cuts asunder and divides, so that it comes into Forms and Images; between these two Properties arises the bitter woe, that is, the sting of Perception and Feeling.

For when there is a motion in the sharpness, then the property is the Aching, and this is also the cause of sensibility and pain; for if there was no sharpness and motion, there would be no sensibility: this motion is also a Ground of the Air in the visible world, which is manifested by the Fire, as shall be mentioned hereafter.

Thus we understand that the Desire is the ground of something, so that something may come out of nothing; and thus we may also conceive that the Desire has been the Beginning of this world, by which God has brought all things into substance and being; for the Desire is that by which God said, *Let there be.* The Desire is that *Fiat*, which has made something where nothing was, but only a Spirit; it has made the *Mysterium Magnum*, which is spiritual, visible, and substantial, as we may see by the Elements, Stars, and other Creatures.

The Second Property, that is, the Motion, was in the beginning of this world the Separator, or Divider in the Powers and Virtues, by which the Creator, namely the Will of God, brought all things out of the *Mysterium Magnum* into form; for it is the outward moveable world, by which the supernatural God made all things, and brought them into form, figure, and shape.

## ☉ *The Third Property.*

The Third Property of the Eternal Nature is the Anguish, namely that Will which has brought itself into the reception to Nature, and something: when the own Will stands in the sharp motion, then it comes into Anguish, that is, into sensibility; for without Nature it is not capable of it, but in the moveable sharpness it comes to be feeling.

And this feeling is the cause of the Fire, and also of the Mind and Senses; for the own natural will is made volatile by it, and seeketh Rest; and thus the separation of the will goes out from itself, and pierces through the Properties, from whence the taste arises, so that one Property tastes and feels the other.

It is also the ground and cause of the Senses, in that one property penetrates into the other, and kindles the other, so that the will knows whence the passiveness comes; for if there was no sensibility, the will could know nothing of the properties, for it would be merely alone: and thus the will receives Nature into it, by feeling the sharp motion in itself.

This motion is in itself like a turning wheel; not that there is such a turning and winding, but it is so in the Properties; for the

Desire attracts into itself, and the motion thrusteth forwards out of itself, and so the will being in this anguish, can neither get inwards nor outwards, and yet is drawn both out of itself and into itself; and so it remains in such a Position, as would go into itself and out of itself, that is, over itself, and under itself, and yet can go no whither, but is an Anguish, and the true foundation of Hell, and of God's Anger; for this Anguish stands in the dark sharp Motion.

In the Creation of the world, the Sulphur-Spirit, with the matter of the Sulphureous Nature, was produced out of this ground; which Sulphur-Spirit is the Natural Life of the Earthly and Elementary Creatures.

The wise Heathen have in some measure understood this ground, for they say, that in *Sulphur*, *Mercury*, and *Sal*, all things in this world consist; wherein they have not looked upon the Matter only, but upon the Spirit, from which such Matter proceeds: for the ground of it consists not in Salt, Quicksilver, and Brimstone, they mean not so, but they mean the Spirit of such Properties; in that every thing indeed consists, whatsoever lives and grows, and has a being in this world, whether it be spiritual or material.

For they understand by *Salt*, the sharp Magnetical Desire of Nature; and by *Mercury*, they mean the Motion and Separation of Nature, by which every thing is figured with its own signature; and by *Sulphur*, they mean the perceiving [sensible] willing, and growing Life.

For in the Sulphur-Spirit, wherein the fiery Life burns, the Oil lies; and the Quintessence lies in the Oil, namely the fiery *Mercury*, which is the true Life of Nature, and which is an Effluence from the word of the Divine Power and Motion, wherein the ground of Heaven is understood; and in the Quintessence there lies the Tincture, namely the Paradisical ground, the outflown word of the Divine power and virtue, wherein the Properties lie in Equality.

Thus, by the Third Property of Nature, which is the Anguish, we mean the sharpness and painfulness of the fire, namely the burning and consuming; for when the will is put into such a sharpness, it will always consume the cause of that sharpness; for it always strives to get to the unity of God again, which is the Rest; and the unity thrusts itself with its Effluence to this motion and sharpness; and so there is a continual conjoining for the manifestation of the Divine will, as we always find in these three, namely in Salt, Brimstone, and Oil, an Heavenly in the Earthly; and whosoever does but truly understand it, and considers the Spirit, shall find it so.

For the soul of a thing lies in the sharpness, and the true life of the sensual Nature and Property lies in the Motion, and the powerful Spirit which arises from the Tincture lies in the Oil of the *Sulphur*: Thus an Heavenly always lies hidden in the Earthly, for the invisible spiritual world came forth with and in the Creation.

## ☉ *The Fourth Property.*

The Fourth Property of the Eternal Nature is the Spiritual Fire, wherein the Light, that is, the Unity, is made manifest; for the Glance of the fire rises and proceeds from the outflown unity, which hath incorporated and united itself with the Natural Desire; and the burning property of fire, namely the Heat, proceeds from the sharp devouring nature of the first three Properties; which comes to be so as follows.

The Eternal Unity, which I also in some of my writings call the Liberty, is the soft and still tranquillity, being amiable, and as a soft comfortable ease, and it cannot be expressed how soft a tranquillity there is without Nature in the Unity of God; but the three Properties in order to Nature are sharp, painful, and horrible.

In these three painful Properties the outflown Will consists, and is produced by the Word or Divine Breathing, and the Unity also is therein; therefore the will longeth earnestly for the Unity, and the Unity longeth for the Sensibility, namely for the fiery ground: thus the one longeth for the other; and when this longing is, there is as it were a cracking noise or flash of Lightning, as when we strike steel and a stone together, or pour water into fire: this we speak by way of similitude.

In that flash the unity feels the sensibility, and the will receives the soft tranquil unity; and so the unity becomes a shining glance of fire, and the fire becomes a burning love, for it receives the *Ens* and power from the soft unity: in this kindling, the darkness of the

Magnetical Compressure is pierced through with the Light, so that it is no more known or discerned, although it remains in itself Eternally in the Compression.

Now two Eternal Principles arise here, namely the darkness, harshness, sharpness, and pain dwelling in itself, and the feeling power and virtue of the unity in the Light; upon which the Scripture saith, that God, that is, the Eternal unity, dwells in a Light to which none can come.

For so the Eternal unity of God manifests itself through the Spiritual Fire in the Light, and this Light is called Majesty; and God, that is, the Supernatural Unity, is the power and virtue of it.

For the Spirit of this Fire receives *Ens* [or virtue] to shine from the unity, or else this fiery ground would be but a painful, horrible hunger, and pricking desire; and it is so indeed, when the will breaks itself off from the unity, and will live after its own desire, as the Devils have done, and the false soul still does.

And thus you may here perceive two Principles: the first is the ground of the burning of the Fire, namely the sharp, moving, perceivable, painful darkness in itself; and the second is the Light of the Fire, wherein the unity comes into mobility and joy; for the Fire is an Object of the great Love of God's unity.

For so the Eternal Delight comes to be perceivable, and this perceiving of the unity is called Love, and is a Burning or Life in the unity of God; and according to this Burning of Love, God calls himself a merciful loving God; for the unity of God loves and pierces through the painful will of the Fire, which at the beginning rose in the breathing of the word, or outgoing of the Divine Delight, and changes it into great Joy.

And in this fiery will of the Eternal Nature stands the soul of Man, and also the Angels; this is their ground and Center; therefore, if any soul breaks itself off from the Light and Love of God, and enters into its own Natural Desire, then the ground of this darkness and painful property will be manifest in it; and this is the hellish Fire, and the Anger of God, when it is made manifest, as may be seen in *Lucifer*; and whatsoever can be thought to have a Being any where in the Creature, the same is likewise without the Creature every where; for the Creature is nothing else but an Image and

Figure of the separable and various power, and virtue of the universal Being.

Now understand right what the ground of Fire is, namely Cold from the Compressure, and Heat from the Anguish; and the Motion is the *Vulcan*; in these three the Fire consists, but the shining of the Light rises and proceeds from the conjunction of the unity in the ground of Fire, and yet the whole ground is but the outflown will.

Therefore in Fire and Light consists the Life of all things, namely in the will thereof, let them be insensible, vegetable, or rational things; every thing as the Fire has its ground, either from the Eternal, as the Soul, or from the Temporary, as Astral Elementary things; for the Eternal is one Fire, and the Temporary is another, as shall be shown hereafter.

## ♀ *The Fifth Property.*

Now the Fifth Property is the Fire of Love, or the World of Power and Light; which in the Darkness dwells in itself, and the Darkness comprehends it not, as it is written, *John* 1. *The Light shines in the Darkness, and the Darkness comprehends it not:* Also, the Word is in the Light, and in the Word is the true understanding Life of Man, namely the true Spirit.

But this Fire is the true Soul of Man, namely the true Spirit, which God breathed into Man for a creaturely Life.

You must understand, in the spiritual Fire of the Will, the true desirous Soul out of the Eternal Ground; and in the power and virtue of the Light, the true understanding Spirit, in which the unity of God dwells and is manifest, as our Lord Christ says, *The Kingdom of God is within you*; and *Paul* saith, *Ye are the temple of the Holy Ghost, who dwells in you*; this is the place of the Divine Inhabitation and Revelation.

Also the Soul comes to be damned thus, when the fiery will breaks itself off from the Love and Unity of God, and enters into its own Natural Propriety, that is, into its Evil Properties: this ought further to be considered.

O Zion, observe this ground, and thou art freed from *Babel*.

The Second Principle (namely the Angelical World and the Thrones) is meant by the Fifth Property: for it is the motion of the unity, wherein all the Properties of the fiery Nature burn in Love.

An Example or similitude of this ground, may be seen in a Candle that is Lighted; the Properties lie in one another in the Candle, and none of them is more manifested than another, till the Candle is lighted, and then we find Fire, Oil, Light, Air and Water from the Air: All the four Elements become manifest in it, which lay hidden before in one only Ground.

And so likewise it must be conceived to be in the Eternal Ground; for the temporary substance is flown from the Eternal, therefore they are both of the same quality; but with this difference, that one is Eternal and the other Transitory, one Spiritual and the other Corporeal.

When the Spiritual Fire and Light shall be kindled, which hath indeed burned from Eternity [in itself], then shall also the Mystery of the Divine Power and Knowledge be always made manifest therein; for all the Properties of the Eternal Nature become spiritual in the Fire, and yet Nature remains as it is, inwardly in itself; and the going forth of the will becomes Spiritual.

For in the crack or flash of the Fire, the dark receptibility is consumed; and in that consuming, the pure bright Fire-Spirit, which is pierced through with the Glance of the Light, goes forth; in which going forth, we find three several Properties.

The first is the going upwards of the fiery will; the second is the going downwards, or sinking of the watery Spirit, namely the Meekness; and the third is the proceeding forwards of the oily Spirit, in the midst, in the Center of the fiery Spirit of the will; which oily Spirit is the *Ens* of the unity of God, which is become a substance in the desire of Nature; yet all is but Spirit and Power: but so it appears in the figure of the Manifestation, not as if there were any separation or division, but it appears so in the Manifestation.

This threefold manifestation is according to the Trinity; for the Center wherein it is, is the only God according to his manifestation: the fiery flaming Spirit of Love is that which goes upwards, and the meekness which proceedeth from the Love, is that which goes downwards, and in the midst there is the Center [of] the circumference, which is the Father, or whole God, according to his manifestation.

And as this is to be known in the Divine manifestation, so it is also in the Eternal Nature, according to Nature's property; for Nature is but a Resemblance of the Diety.

Nature may be further considered thus: the flash of the Original of fire, is a crack, and salnitrous ground, whence Nature goes forth into infinite divisions, that is, into multitudes or varieties of Powers and Virtues; from which the multitude of Angels and Spirits, and their colours and operations, proceeded, also the four Elements in the beginning of time.

For the temperature of Fire and Light is the holy Element, namely the motion in the Light of the unity; and from this salnitrous ground (we mean spiritual, not earthly salnitre) the four Elements proceed, namely in the compressure of the fiery *Mercury*, Earth and Stones are produced; and in the Quintessence of the fiery *Mercury*, the Fire and Heaven; and in the Motion or proceeding forth, the Air; and in the diruption or rending of the Desire by the Fire, the water is produced.

The fiery *Mercury* is a dry water, that has brought forth Metals and Stones; but the broken or divided *Mercury* has brought forth moist water, by the Mortification in the Fire; and the compression has brought the gross rawness into the Earth, which is a gross salnitrous Saturnine *Mercury*.

By the word *Mercury*, you must understand, here in the Spirit, always the outflown Natural working word of God, which has been the Separator, Divider, and Former of every substance; and by the word *Saturn*, we mean the compression.

In the fifth Property, that is, in the Light, the Eternal unity is substantial; that is, an holy Spiritual Fire, an holy Light, an holy Air, which is nothing else but Spirit, also an holy water, which is the outflowing Love of the unity of God, and an holy Earth, which is all-powerful virtue and working.

This fifth Property is the true spiritual Angelical world of the Divine joy, which is hidden in this visible world.

# 2. *The Sixth Property.*

The Sixth Property of the Eternal Nature, is the sound, noise, voice, or understanding; for when the Fire flashes, all the Properties together sound: the Fire is the mouth of the Essence, the Light is the Spirit, and the Sound is the Understanding, wherein all the Properties understand one another.

According to the Manifestation of the Holy Trinity, by the Effluence of the unity, this sound or voice is the Divine working word, namely the understanding in the Eternal Nature, by which the supernatural knowledge manifests itself; but according to Nature and Creature, this sound or voice is the knowledge of God, wherein the Natural understanding knows God; for the Natural understanding is a Model, Resemblance, and Effluence from the Divine understanding.

The five Senses lie in the Natural understanding, in a Spiritual manner, and in the second Property, namely in the motion, in the fiery *Mercury*, they lie in a Natural manner.

The sixth Property gives understanding in the voice or sound, namely in the speaking of the word; and the second property of Nature is the producer, and also the House, Tool, or Instrument of the speech or voice: in the second Property, the Power and Virtue is painful; but in the sixth Property, it is joyful and pleasant; and the difference between the second and sixth Property, is in Light and Darkness, which are in one another, as Fire and Light; there is no other difference between them.

# ) *The Seventh Property.*

The Seventh Property is the Substance, that is, the *subjectum*, or house of the other six, in which they all are substantially as the soul in the body: by this we understand especially, as to the Light world, the Paradise or budding of the working Power.

For every Property makes unto itself a Subject, or Object, by its own Effluence; and in the seventh, all the Properties are in a temperature, as in one only Substance: and as they all proceeded from the unity, so they all return again into one ground.

And though they work in different kinds and manners, yet here there is but one only Substance, whose power and virtue is called Tincture; that is, an holy penetrating, growing, or springing Bud.

Not that the seventh Property is the Tincture, but it is the Body of it; the Power and Virtue of the Fire and Light, is the Tincture in the substantial Body: but the seventh Property is the substance which the Tincture penetrates and sanctifies; we mean, that it is thus according to the power and virtue of the Divine manifestation; but as it is a Property of Nature, it is the substance of the attracted desire of all properties.

It is especially to be observed, that always the First and the Seventh Property are accounted for one; and the Second and Sixth; also the Third and Fifth; and the Fourth is only the dividing Mark or bound.

For according to the manifestation of the Trinity of God, there are but three Properties of Nature: the first is the Desire which belongs to God the Father, yet it is only a Spirit; but in the seventh Property, the Desire is substantial.

The second is the Divine power and virtue, and belongs to God the Son; in the second Number it is only a Spirit; but in the sixth it is the substantial Power and Virtue.

The third belongs to the Holy Ghost; and in the beginning of the third Property it is only a fiery Spirit; but in the fifth Property, the great Love is manifested therein.

Thus the Effluence of the Divine Manifestation, as to the three Properties in the first Principle before the Light, is Natural; but in the second Principle in the Light, it is Spiritual.

Now these are the seven Properties in one only Ground; and all seven are equally Eternal without beginning; none of them can be accounted the first, second, third, fourth, fifth, sixth, or last; for they are equally Eternal without beginning, and have also one Eternal beginning from the unity of God.

We must represent this in a typical way, that it may be understood how the one is born out of the other, the better to conceive what the Creator is, and what the Life and Substance of this world is.

## The Seven Forms of Spirits, mentioned Revel. Chap. 1.

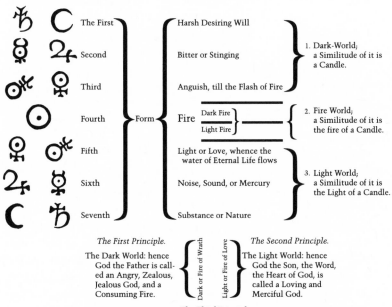

*The First Principle.*

The Dark World: hence
God the Father is call-
ed an Angry, Zealous,
Jealous God, and a
Consuming Fire.

{ Dark or Fire of Wrath | Light or Fire of Love }

*The Second Principle.*

The Light World: hence
God the Son, the Word,
the Heart of God, is
called a Loving and
Merciful God.

*The Third Principle.*

This World of four Elements, which is produced out of the two Inward Worlds,
and is a Glass of them, wherein Light and Darkness, Good and Evil are mixed, it is
not Eternal, but has a Beginning and an End.

# Of the Third Principle, namely The visible World; whence that proceeded; and what the Creator is.

T H I S visible world is sprung from the spiritual world before mentioned, namely from the outflown Divine Power and Virtue; and it is a Subject or Object resembling the spiritual world: the spiritual world is the Inward ground of the visible world; the visible subsists in the spiritual.

The visible world is only an Effluence of the seven Properties, for it proceeded out of the six working Properties; but in the seventh (that is, in Paradise), it is in Rest: and that is the Eternal Sabbath of Rest, wherein the Divine Power and Virtue rests.

*Moses* saith, God created Heaven and Earth, and all Creatures, in six Days, and rested on the seventh Day, and also commanded it to be kept for a Rest.

The understanding lies hidden and secret in those words: could not he have made all his works in one Day? Neither can we properly say there was any day before the Sun was; for in the Deep there is but one Day [in all].

But the understanding lies hidden in those words: he understands by each day's working, the Creation, or Manifestation of the seven Properties; for he saith, In the Beginning God created Heaven and Earth.

In the FIRST Motion, the Magnetical Desire compressed and compacted the fiery and watery *Mercury* with the other Properties; and then the grossness separated itself from the Spiritual Nature: and the fiery became Metals and Stones, and partly Salnitre, that is, Earth: and the watery became water: then the fiery *Mercury* of the working became clean, and *Moses* calls it Heaven; and the Scripture says, God dwells in Heaven: for this fiery *Mercury* is the Power and Virtue of the Firmament, namely an Image and resemblance of the Spiritual world, in which God is manifested.

When this was done, God said, Let there be Light; then the

Inward thrust itself forth through the fiery Heaven, from which a shining power and virtue arose in the fiery *Mercury*, and that was the Light of the outward Nature in the Properties, wherein the vegetable Life consists.

## The Second Day.

In the SECOND Day's work, God separated the watery and fiery *Mercury* from one another, and called the fiery the Firmament of Heaven, which came out of the midst of the waters, namely of *Mercury*, whence arose the Male and Female kind, in the Spirit of the outward world; that is, the Male in the fiery *Mercury*, and the Female in the watery.

This Separation was made all over in every thing, to the end that the fiery *Mercury* should desire and long for the watery, and the watery for the fiery; that so there might be a Desire of Love betwixt them in the Light of Nature, from which the Conjunction arises: therefore the fiery *Mercury*, namely the outflown word, separated itself according both to the fiery and to the watery nature of the Light, and thence comes both the Male and Female kind in all things, both Animals and Vegetables.

## The Third Day.

In the THIRD Day's work, the fiery and watery *Mercury* entered again into Conjunction or Mixture, and embraced one another, wherein the Salnitre, namely the Separator in the Earth, brought forth Grass, Plants, and Trees; and that was the first Generation or production between Male and Female.

## The Fourth Day.

In the FOURTH Day's work, the fiery *Mercury* brought forth its fruit, namely the fifth Essence, an higher power or virtue of Life, than the four Elements, and yet it is in the Elements: of it the Stars are made.

For as the compression of the Desire brought the Earth into a

Mass, the compression entering into itself, so the fiery *Mercury* thrust itself outwards by the Compression, and has inclosed the place of this world with the Stars and starry Heaven.

## The Fifth Day.

In the FIFTH Day's work, the *Spiritus Mundi*, that is, the soul of the great world, opened itself in the fifth Essence (we mean the Life of the fiery and watery *Mercury*); therein God created all beasts, fishes, fowls, and worms; every one from its peculiar property of the divided *Mercury*.

Here we see how the Eternal Principles have moved themselves according to Evil and Good, as to all the seven Properties, and their Effluence and Mixture; for there are evil and good Creatures created, every thing as the *Mercury* (that is, the Separator) has figured and framed himself into an *Ens*, as may be seen in the evil and good Creatures: And yet every kind of Life has its Original in the Light of Nature, that is, in the Love of Nature; from which it is that all Creatures, in their Kind or Property, love one another according to this outflown Love.

## The Sixth Day.

In the SIXTH Day's work, God created Man; for in the sixth Day the understanding of Life opened itself out of the fiery *Mercury*, that is, out of the Inward Ground.

God created him in his likeness out of all the three Principles, and made him an Image, and breathed into him the understanding fiery *Mercury*, according to both the Inward and Outward Ground, that is, according to Time and Eternity, and so he became a living understanding soul: and in this Ground of the soul, the Manifestation of the Divine Holiness moved, namely the living outflowing word of God, together with the Eternal knowing *Idea*, which was known from Eternity in the Divine Wisdom, as a Subject or Form of the Divine Imagination.

This *Idea* becomes clothed with the Substance of the heavenly world, and so it becomes an understanding Spirit and Temple of

God; an Image of the Divine vision, which Spirit is given to the Soul for a Spouse: as Fire and Light are espoused together, so it is here also to be understood.

This Divine Ground budded and pierced through soul and body; and this was the true Paradise in Man, which he lost by sin, when the ground of the dark world, with the false Desire, got the upper hand and dominion in him.

## The Seventh Day.

In the SEVENTH Day God rested from all his works which he had made, saith *Moses*; yet God needs no Rest, for he has wrought from Eternity, and he is a mere working Power and Virtue; therefore the meaning and understanding here lies hidden in the Word, for *Moses* saith he hath commanded [us] to Rest on the seventh Day.

The seventh Day was the true Paradise, understand it spiritually, that is, the Tincture of the Divine Power and Virtue, which is a temperament; this pierced through all the Properties, and wrought in the seventh, that is, in the substance of all the others.

The Tincture pierced through the Earth, and through all Elements, and tinctured All; and then Paradise was on Earth, and in Man; for evil was hidden: as the Night is hidden in the Day, so the wrath of Nature was also hidden in the first Principle, till the fall of Man; and then the Divine working, with the Tincture, fled into their own Principle, namely into the Inward Ground of the Light-world.

For the wrath rose aloft, and got the predominancy, and that is the Curse, where it is said, God cursed the Earth; for his cursing is to leave off and fly from his working: as when God's Power and Virtue in a thing works with the Life and Spirit of the thing, and afterwards withdraws itself with its working; then the thing is cursed, for it works in its own will, and not in God's will.

## Of the Spiritus Mundi, and of the Four Elements.

We may very well observe and consider the hidden spiritual world, by the visible world: for we see that Fire, Light, and Air, are continually begotten in the deep of this world; and that there is no Rest or Cessation from this production; and that it has been so from the beginning of the world; and yet men can find no cause of it in the outward world, or tell what the ground of it should be: but Reason says, God hath so created it, and therefore it continues so; which indeed is true in itself; but Reason knows not the Creator, which thus creates without ceasing; that is, the true *Archaeus*, or Separator, which is an Effluence out of the Invisible world, namely the outflown word of God; which I mean and understand by the word fiery *Mercury*.

For what the invisible world is, in a spiritual working, where Light and Darkness are in one another, and yet the one not comprehending the other, that the visible world is, in a substantial working; whatsoever powers and virtues in the outflown word are to be understood in the Inward Spiritual world, the same we understand also in the visible world, in the Stars and Elements, yet in another Principle of a more holy Nature.

The four Elements flow from the *Archaeus* of the Inward ground, that is, from the four Properties of the Eternal Nature, and were in the beginning of time so outbreathed from the Inward ground, and compressed and formed into a working substance and life; and therefore the outward world is called a Principle, and is a subject of the Inward world, that is, a Tool and Instrument of the Inward Master, which Master is the Word and Power of God.

And as the Inward Divine world has in it an understanding Life from the Effluence of the Divine knowledge, whereby the Angels and Souls are meant; so likewise the outward world has a Rational Life in it, consisting in the outflown powers and virtues of the Inward world; which outward [Rational] Life has no higher understanding and can reach no further than that thing wherein it dwells, namely the Stars and four Elements.

The *Spiritus Mundi* is hidden in the four Elements, as the Soul is in the body, and is nothing else but an Effluence and working Power proceeding from the Sun and Stars; its dwelling wherein it works is spiritual, encompassed with the four Elements.

The Spiritual house is first a sharp Magnetical power and virtue, from the Effluence of the Inward world, from the first property of the Eternal Nature; this is the ground of all salt and powerful virtue, also of all forming and substantiality.

Secondly, it is the Effluence of the Inward Motion, which is outflown from the second form of the Eternal Nature, and consists in a fiery Nature, like a dry kind of water source, which is understood to be the ground of all Metal and Stones, for they were created of that.

I call it the fiery *Mercury* in the Spirit of this world, for it is the mover of all things, and the separator of the powers and virtues; a former of all shapes, a ground of the outward Life, as to the Motion and Sensibility.

The third ground is the perception in the Motion and Sharpness, which is a spiritual source of Sulphur, proceeding from the ground of the painful will in the Inward ground: Hence the Spirit with the five senses arise, namely seeing, hearing, feeling, tasting, and smelling; and this is the true Essential Life, whereby the fire, that is, the fourth form, is made manifest.

The ancient wise men have called these three properties *Sulphur*, *Mercurius*, and *Sal*, as to their Materials which were produced thereby in the four Elements, into which this Spirit does coagulate, or make itself Substantial.

The four Elements lie also in this ground, and are nothing different or separate from it; they are only the manifestation of this spiritual ground, and are as a dwelling place of the Spirit, in which this Spirit works.

The Earth is the grossest Effluence from this subtle Spirit; after the Earth the Water is the second; after the Water the Air is the Third; and after the Air the Fire is the fourth: All these proceed from one only ground, namely from the *Spiritus Mundi*, which has its root in the Inward world.

But Reason will say, To what End has the Creator made this manifestation? I answer, There is no other cause, but that the spiritual world might thereby bring itself into a visible form or Image, that the Inward powers and virtues might have a form and Image: Now that this might be, the spiritual substance must needs bring itself into a material ground, wherein it may so figure and form itself; and there must be such a separation, as that this separated being might continually long for the first ground again, namely the Inward for the Outward, and the Outward for the Inward.

So also the four Elements, which are nothing else Inwardly but one only Ground, must long one for the other, and desire one another, and seek the Inward Ground in one another.

For the Inward Element in them is divided, and the four Elements are but the Properties of that divided Element, and that causes the great anxiety and desire betwixt them; they desire continually [to get] into the first ground again, that is, into that one Element in which they may rest; of which the Scripture speaks, saying: *Every Creature groaneth with us, and earnestly longs to be delivered from the vanity, which it is subject to against its will.*

In this anxiety and desire, the Effluence of the Divine power and virtue, by the working of Nature, is together also formed and brought into figures, to the Eternal Glory and Contemplation of Angels and Men, and all Eternal Creatures; as we may see clearly in all living things, and also in vegetables, how the Divine power and virtue imprints and forms itself.

For there is not any thing substantial in this world, wherein the image, resemblance, and form of the Inward spiritual world does not stand; whether it be according to the wrath of the Inward ground, or according to the good virtue; and yet in the most venomous virtue or quality, in the Inward ground, many times there lies the greatest virtue out of the Inward world.

But where there is a dark Life, that is, a dark Oil, in a thing, there is little to be expected from it; for it is the foundation of the wrath, namely a false bad Poison, to be utterly rejected.

Yet where Life consists in venom, and has a Light or Brightness shining in the Oil, namely in the Fifth Essence, therein Heaven is manifested in Hell, and a great virtue lies hidden it it: this is understood by those that are ours.

The whole visible world is a mere spermatical working ground; every thing has an inclination and longing towards another, the uppermost towards the undermost, and the undermost towards the uppermost, for they are separated one from the other; and in this hunger they embrace one another in the Desire.

As we may know by the Earth, which is so very hungry after the [influence and virtue of the] Stars, and the *Spiritus Mundi*, namely after the Spirit from whence it proceeded in the beginning, that it has no rest for hunger; and this hunger of the Earth consumes Bodies, that the Spirit may be parted again from the gross Elementary condition, and return into its *Archaeus* again.

Also we see in this hunger the Impregnation of the *Archaeus*, that is, of the Separator, how the undermost *Archaeus* of the Earth attracts the outermost subtle *Archaeus* from the Constellations above the Earth; where this compacted Ground from the uppermost *Archaeus* longs for its ground again, and puts itself forth towards the uppermost; in which putting forth, the growing of Metals, Plants and Trees, has its original.

For the *Archaeus* of the Earth becomes thereby exceedingly joyful, because it tastes and feels its first ground in itself again, and in this Joy all things spring out of the Earth, and therein also the growing of Animals consists, namely in a continual Conjunction of the Heavenly and Earthly, in which the Divine power and virtue also works, as may be known by the Tincture of the Vegetables in their Inward ground.

Therefore Man, who is so noble an Image, having his ground in Time and Eternity, should well consider himself, and not run headlong in such blindness, seeking his Native Country afar off from himself, when it is within himself, though covered with the grossness of the Elements by their strife.

Now when the strife of the Elements ceases, by the Death of the gross body, then the Spiritual Man will be made manifest, whether he be born in and to Light, or Darkness; which of these [two] bears the Sway, and has the Dominion in him, the Spiritual Man has his being in it Eternally, whether it be in the foundation of God's Anger, or in his Love.

For the outward visible Man is not now the Image of God, it is nothing but an Image of the *Archaeus*, that is, a house [or husk] of the Spiritual Man, in which the Spiritual Man grows, as Gold does in the gross Stone, and a Plant from the wild Earth; as the Scripture says, *as we have a Natural Body, so we have also a Spiritual Body: such as the Natural is, such also is the Spiritual.*

The outward gross Body of the four Elements shall not inherit the Kingdom of God, but that which is born out of that one Element, namely out of the Divine Manifestation and Working.

For this Body of the Flesh and of the Will of Man is not it, but that which is wrought by the heavenly *Archaeus* in this gross Body, unto which this gross [Body] is a house, tool, and instrument.

But when the Crust is taken away, then it shall appear why we have here been called Men; and yet some of us have scarce been Beasts; nay, some far worse than Beasts.

For we should rightly consider what the Spirit of the outward world is; it is a house's husk, and Instrument of the Inward Spiritual world which is hidden in it, and works through it, and so brings itself into Figures and Images.

And thus human Reason is but a house of the true understanding of the Divine knowledge: none should trust so much in his reason and sharp wit, for it is but the Constellation of the outward Stars, and rather seduces him, than leads him to the unity of God.

Reason must wholly yield itself up to God, that the Inward *Archaeus* may be revealed; and this shall work and bring forth a true Spiritual understanding ground, uniform with God, in which God's Spirit will be revealed, and will bring the understanding to God: and then, in this Ground, *the Spirit searches through all things, even the deep things of God,* as St. *Paul* saith.

I thought good to set this down thus briefly for the Lovers, for their further consideration.

## Now follows a short Explanation, or Description of the Divine Manifestation.

God is the Eternal, Immense, Incomprehensible unity, which manifests itself in itself, from Eternity in Eternity, by the Trinity; and is Father, Son, and Holy Ghost, in a threefold working, as is before mentioned.

The first Effluence and manifestation of this Trinity is the Eternal word, or outspeaking of the Divine power and virtue.

The first outspoken Substance from that Power is the Divine wisdom; which is a substance wherein the Power works.

Out of the wisdom flows the Power and Virtue of the breathing forth, and goes into separability and forming; and therein the Divine Power is manifest in its virtue.

These separable Powers and Virtues bring themselves into the power of reception, to their own perceptibility; and out of the perceptibility arises own self-will and Desire: this own Will is the Ground of the Eternal Nature, and it brings itself, with the Desire, into the Properties as far as Fire.

In the Desire, is the Original of Darkness; and in the Fire, the Eternal unity is made manifest with the Light, in the fiery Nature.

Out of this fiery Property, and the property of the Light, the Angels and Souls have their Original; which is a Divine Manifestation.

The Power and Virtue of Fire and Light is called Tincture; and the Motion of this Virtue is called the holy and Pure Element.

The Darkness becomes substantial in itself; and the Light becomes also substantial in the fiery Desire: these two make two Principles, namely God's Anger in the Darkness, and God's Love in the Light; each of them works in itself, and there is only such a difference between them, as between Day and Night, and yet both of them have but one only Ground; and the one is always a cause of the other, and that the other becomes manifest and known in it, as Light from Fire.

The visible world is the third Principle, that is, the third Ground and beginning: this is breathed out of the Inward Ground, namely out of both the first Principles, and brought into the Nature and Form of a Creature.

The Inward Eternal working is hidden in the visible world; and it is in every thing, and through every thing, yet not to be comprehended by any thing in the Thing's own Power; the outward Powers and Virtues are but passive, and the house in which the Inward work.

All the other worldly Creatures are but the Substance of the outward World, but Man, who is created both out of Time and Eternity, out of the Being of all Beings, and made an Image of the Divine manifestation.

The Eternal Manifestation of the Divine Light is called the Kingdom of Heaven, and the Habitation of the Holy Angels and Souls.

The fiery Darkness is called Hell, or God's Anger, wherein the Devils dwell, together with the damned Souls.

In the place of this World, Heaven and Hell are present every where, but according to the Inward Ground.

Inwardly, the Divine working is manifest in God's Children; but in the wicked, the working of the painful darkness.

The place of the Eternal Paradise is hidden in this World, in the Inward Ground; but manifest in the Inward Man, in which God's Power and Virtue works.

There shall perish of this World only the four Elements, together with the Starry Heaven, and the Earthly Creatures, namely the outward gross life of all things.

The Inward Power and Virtue of every substance remains Eternally.

## Another Explanation of the Mysterium Magnum.

God has manifested the *Mysterium Magnum* out of the Power and Virtue of his word; in which *Mysterium Magnum* the whole Creation has lain essentially without forming, in *Temperamento*; and by which he has outspoken the Spiritual formings in Separablility [or variety]: in which formings, the Sciences of the Powers and Virtues in the Desire, that is, in the *Fiat*, have stood, wherein every Science, in the Desire to Manifestation, has brought itself into a Corporeal Substance.

Such a *Mysterium Magnum* lies also in Man, namely in the Image of God, and is the Essential word of the Power of God, according to Time and Eternity, by which the Living word of God speaketh forth, or expresses itself, either in Love or Anger, or in Fancy, all as the *Mysterium* stands in a moveable Desire to Evil or Good; according to that saying, such as the people is, such a God they also have.

For in whatsoever property the *Mysterium* in Man is awakened, such a word also utters itself from his powers: as we plainly see that nothing else but vanity is uttered by the wicked. *Praise the Lord, all ye his Works. Hallelujah.*

## Of the Word  S C I E N C E.

The word Science is not so taken by me as men understand the word *Scientia* in the *Latin* Tongue; for I understand therein even the true Ground according to Sense, which, both in the *Latin* and all other Languages, is missed and neglected by Ignorance; for every word in its impressure, forming, and Expression, gives the true understanding of what that thing is that is so called.

You understand by Science some skill or knowledge, in which you say true, but do not fully express the meaning.

Science is the Root to the Understanding, as to the Sensibility; it is the Root to the Center of the Impressure of nothing into something; as when the Will of the Abyss attracts itself into itself, to a Center of the Impressure, namely to the Word, then arises the true Understanding.

The Will is in the Separability of the Science, and there separates itself out from the Impressed Compaction; and men first of all understand the Essence in that which is separated, in which the Separability impresses itself into a Substance.

For Essence is a substantial power and virtue, but Science is a moving unsettled one, like the Senses; it is indeed the Root of the Senses.

Yet in the Understanding, in which it is called Science, it is not the perception, but a cause of the perception, in that manner as when the Understanding impresses itself in the Mind, there must first be a cause which must give the Mind, from which the Understanding flows forth into its Contemplation: Now this Science is the Root to the fiery Mind, and it is in short the Root of all Spiritual Beginnings; it is the true Root of Souls, and proceeds through every Life, for it is the Ground from whence Life comes.

I could not give it any better Name, this does so wholly accord and agree in the Sense; for the Science is the cause that the Divine Abyssal Will compacts and impresses itself into Nature, to the

separable, [various] intelligible, and perceivable Life of understanding and difference; for from the Impressure of the Science, whereby
the Will attracts it into itself, the Natural Life arises, and the Word
of every Life Originally.

The distinction or separation out of the Fire is to be understood
as follows: The Eternal Science in the Will of the Father draws the
Will, which is called Father, into itself, and shuts itself into a
Center of the Divine Generation of the Trinity, and by the Science
speaks itself forth into a word of understanding; and in the Speaking
is the Separation in the Science; and in every Separation there is the
Desire to the Impression of the Expression, the Impression is
Essential, and is called Divine Essence.

From this Essence the word expresses itself in the second
Separation, that is, of Nature, and in that expression wherein the
Natural Will separates itself in its Center, into a preception, the
Separation out of the fiery Science is understood; for thence comes
the Soul and all Angelical Spirits.

The third Separation is according to the outward Nature of the
expressed formed Word, wherein the Bestial Science lies, as may be
seen in the Treatise of the *Election of Grace*, which has a sharp
understanding, and is one of the Clearest of our Writings.

## *FINIS.*

A N

# ILLUSTRATION

O F   T H E

# DEEP PRINCIPLES

O F

JACOB BEHMEN, the Teutonic Theosopher,

IN THIRTEEN FIGURES,

Left by DIONYSIUS ANDREW FREHER.

# NUMBER I.

G O D, without all Nature and Creature.

The Unformed Word in Trinity without all Nature. *Vid. et N.B. Mysterium Magnum,* iv. 3.

A and Ω; the Eternal Beginning and the Eternal End, the First and the Last.

The greatest Softness, Meekness, Stillness, etc.

Nothing and All. Eternal Liberty.

Abyss, without Ground, Time, and Place.

The Still Eternity. *Mysterium Magnum* without Nature. Chaos.

The Mirror of Wonders, or Wonderful Eye of Eternity.

The first Temperature, or Temperature in Nothingness; a Calm, Serene Habitation, but without all Luster and Glory.

The Trinity Unmanifest, or rather, that Triune Unsearchable Being, which cannot be an Object of any created Understanding.

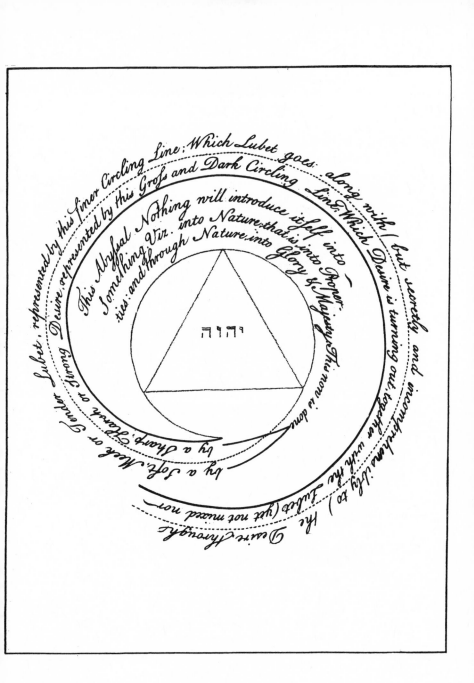

# NUMBER II.

The three first. (Sal, Sulphur, and Mercury.)

The Triangle in Nature.

The inferior, restless Part of Nature.

The Properties of Darkness. The Root of Fire.

The Wheel of Nature.

The three Properties on the Left Hand, appropriable in Sense unto the Father, Son, and Spirit.

The Hellish World, if in a Creature divorced from the Three on the Right.

*N. B.* Virgin . . . Opposite to what in the Light World is called Virgin Wisdom.

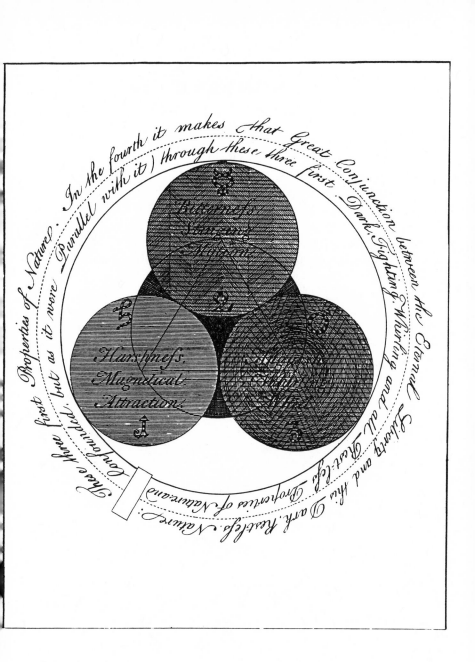

In the fourth it makes that Great Conjunction between the Eternal Liberty and the Dark Restless Properties of Nature: and as it were Parallel with it) through these three first. Dark Fighting, Whirling and all the three first Properties of Nature. These three first Confounded.

Bitterness Stinging Motion

Harshness Magnetical Attraction

# NUMBER III.

The Fourth Property of Eternal Nature.
The Magic Fire. The Fire World.
The First Principle.
The Generation of the Cross.
The Strength, Might and Power of Eternal Nature.
The Abyss's or Eternal Liberty's Opening in the dark World, breaking and consuming all the strong Attraction of Darkness.

The Distinguishing Mark, standing in the Midst between three and three, looking with the first terrible Crack (made in the first, gross and rough Hardness) into the Dark World; and with the second joyful Crack (made in the second, soft, watery or conquered Hardness) into the Light World; and giving unto each what it is capable of, namely Might, Strength, Terror, etc. unto the former, but Light, Splendor, Luster and Glory, unto the latter.

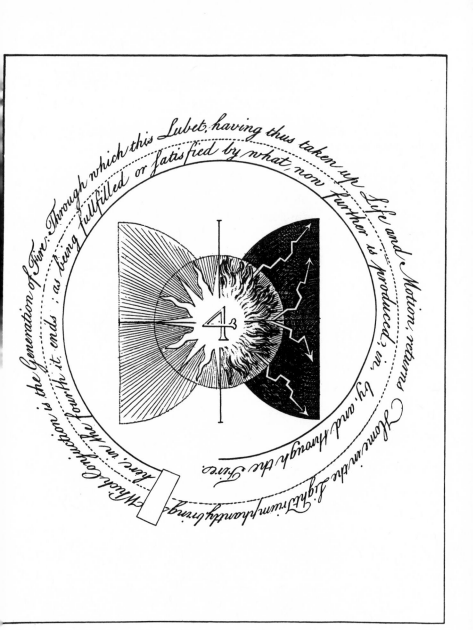

Which Conjunction is the Generation of Fire. Through which this Lubet, having thus taken up Life and Motion, returns Home in the Light triumphantly burning here, in the fourth it ends; as being fulfilled or satisfied by what, now further is produced; in by, and through the Fire.

# NUMBER IV.

The three Exalted, Tinctured, or Transmuted Properties on the Right Hand. The Kingdom of Love, Light, and Glory.

The Second Principle.

The Second Temperature, or Temperature in Substantiality.

The Trinity manifested, which only now can be an Object of a created Understanding. Byss. Wisdom. Tincture.

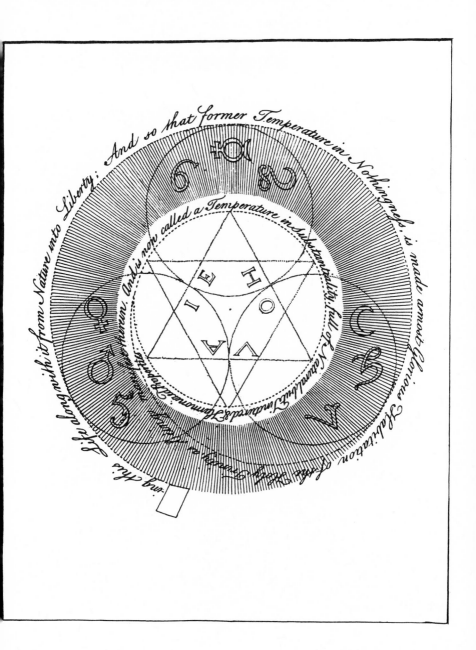

# NUMBER V.

The four first Figures were, in some Manner, to show (according to the deep and wonderful Manifestation of the Divine Spirit, given to *Jacob Behmen*) the Generation of Eternal Nature, which has a Beginning without Beginning, and an End without End.

This fifth represents now, that this great Royal Residence, or Divine Habitation of Glory, of GOD the Father, GOD the Son, and GOD the Holy Ghost, was replenished at once with innumerable Inhabitants, All Glorious Flames of Fire, All Children of GOD, and All Ministering Spirits, divided in three Hierarchies (each of such an Extent, that no Limits can be perceived, and yet not infinite) according to that Holy Number Three. But we know the Names only of two of them, which are *Michael* and *Uriel*, because only these two, with all their Hosts, kept their Habitation in the Light.

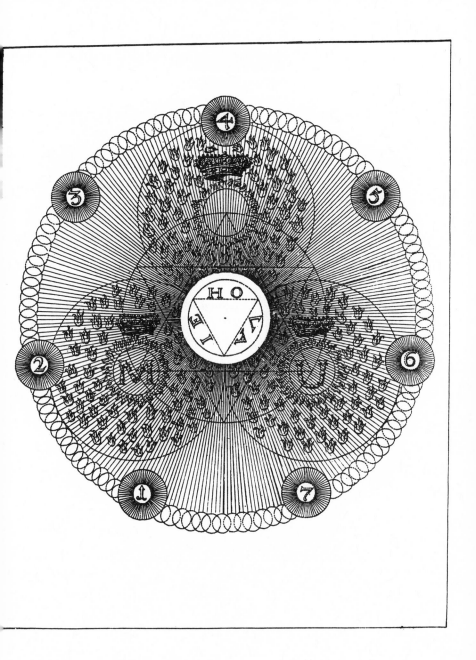

# NUMBER VI.

Here now one of those three Hierarchs, even the most glorious of them, because he was the Created Representative of GOD the Son, commits High Treason, revolts, lets his dark, proud Will-Spirit, in a false *Magia*, without any Occasion given him from without, out of his own Center fly up on high, above God and all the Hosts of Heaven, to be himself All in All; but he is resisted, and precipitated down, and falls through the Fire into eternal Darkness, in which he is a mighty Prince over his own Legions, but in Reality a poor Prisoner, and an infamous Executioner of the Wrath of God; and may now well be reproached, and asked, How art thou fallen from Heaven, O *Lucifer*, Son of the Morning? To which Question a profound, prolix, distinct, most particular and circumstantial Answer is given, in the *Aurora*, to his eternal Shame and Confusion, which he had hid and covered from the Beginning of the World.

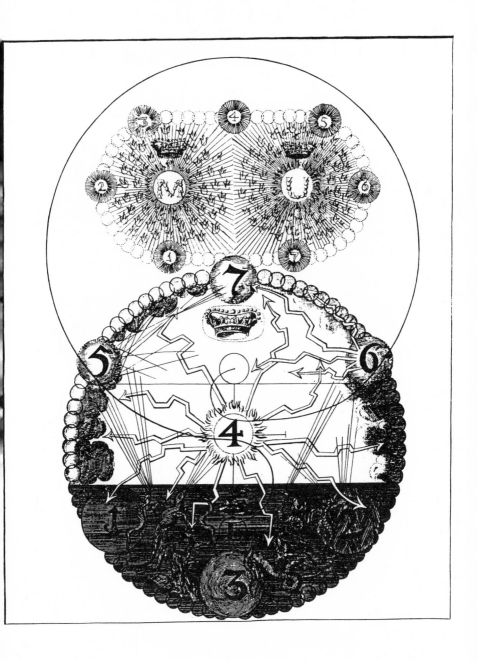

# NUMBER VII.

When *Lucifer* by his Rebellion had brought the whole Extent of his Kingdom into such a desolate Condition, that it was, as *Moses* describes it, without Form and Void, and Darkness was upon the Face of the Deep, that whole Region was justly taken away from under his Dominion, and transformed into such another meaner and temporary Condition, that it could no more be of any Use to him. And when this was fully settled in Six Days Time, according to the Six Active Spirits of eternal Nature, so that it wanted nothing more but a Prince and Ruler, instead of him who had forsaken his Habitation in the Light, *ADAM* was created in the Image and Likeness of GOD, an Epitome, or Compendium of the whole Universe, by the *VERBUM FIAT*, which was the Eternal Word, in Conjunction with the first Astringent Fountain-Spirit of Eternal Nature.

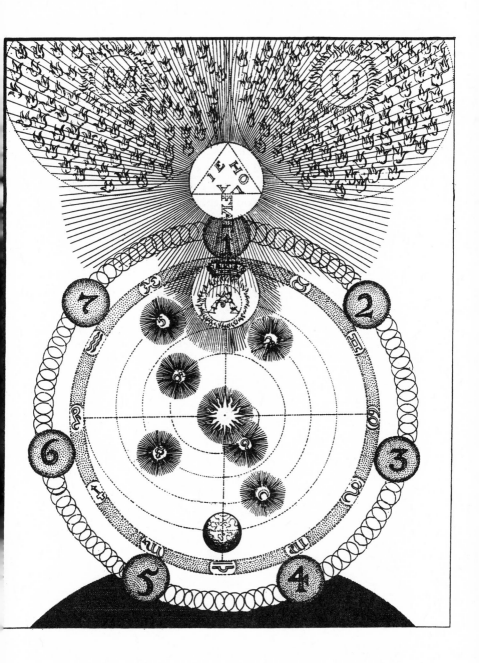

# NUMBER VIII.

This *ADAM*, though he was indeed created in a State of Innocence, Purity, Integrity, and Perfection, could not yet stand on that Top of Perfection which he was designed for, and would have been drawn up into, if he had stood his Trial, for which there was an absolute Necessity. Three Things there were that laid a Claim to *Adam*, and though they stood within him in an equal Temperature, yet did they not so without him, for *Lucifer* had made a Breach.

These three Things were, (1) above him *SOPHIA*, called (*Mal.* ii. 14.) his Companion, and the Wife of his Youth. (2) SATAN, that uncreated dark Root in the Beginningless Beginning of eternal Nature. And (3) The SPIRIT OF THIS WORLD. And herein lies the Ground of the Necessity of *Adam*'s Temptation.

In this Consideration the Devil comes not yet in, though he is not far out of the Way; nor the Tree of Knowledge of Good and Evil; because this was but a necessary Consequence of *Adam*'s wavering, and dealing treacherously with the Wife of his Youth.

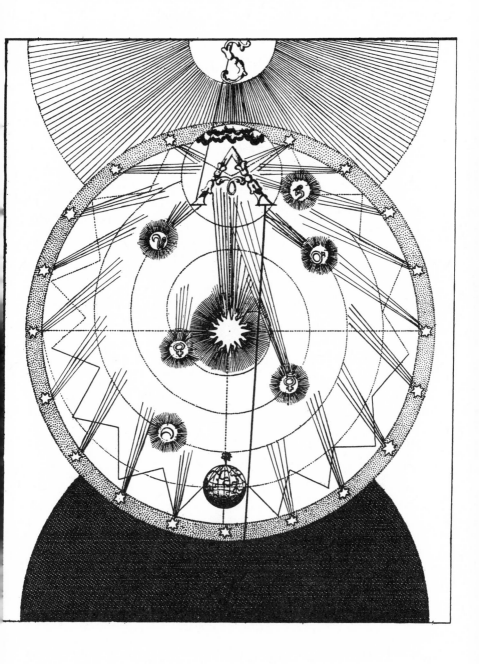

# NUMBER IX.

Here now is poor *Adam* actually fallen away from all his former Happiness and Glory, and has lost whatsoever was good and desirable both in himself and round about him: He lies as dead, on the outmost Borders of the Spirit of this World. *SOPHIA* has forsaken him, or rather he, having dealt treacherously, has forsaken Her, and the Holy Band of the Marriage-Covenant that was between them is dissolved: He is all over dark, and lies even under the Earth, over which he was to rule: All the Stars shoot their Influences upon him, of which the very best are but Death and Poison to that Life for which he was created: And nothing less could he expect, but that every Moment he should be quite drawn down and swallowed up in the Belly of Satan. This was his State and Condition after his Transgression, and before he heard the Word of Free Grace, *that the Woman's Seed should bruise the Serpent's Head.*

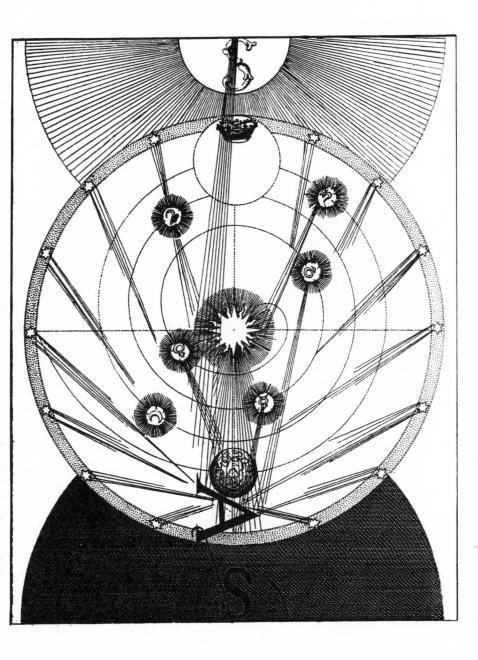

# NUMBER X.

Here *Adam*, by that Word of Grace treasured up in his Heart, whose Name is JESUS, is raised again so far, that he can stand above the Earthly Globe, upon the Basis of a fiery Triangle △ which is an excellent Emblem of his own Soul, and the Holy Name JESUS stands above him upon the Top of a watery Triangle. ▽ and these two Triangles, which in *Adam*'s Fall were divorced from each other, do now touch each other again, though (in this Beginning) but in one Point; that the Soul's Desire may draw down into itself the ▽ and that Holy Name may draw up into itself more and more the △ till these two make up a complete ✡ the most significant Character in all the Universe: For only then the Work of Regeneration and Reunion with *SOPHIA* will be absolved. And although, during this mortal Life, no such Perfection of the whole Man can be wrought out, yet is it attainable in the inward Part; and whatsoever seems to be an Obstruction (even SIN NOT EX-CEPTED), must, for this very End, WORK TOGETHER FOR GOOD TO THEM THAT LOVE GOD. Praised be his Triune Holy, Holy, Holy Name, in this Time, and throughout all the Extent and Duration of Eternity.

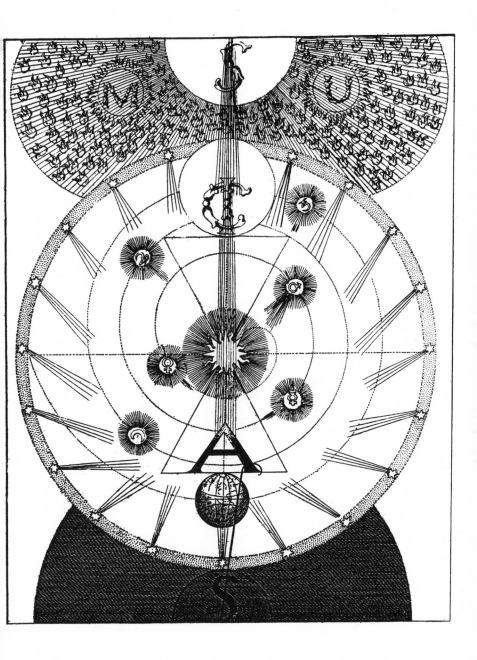

# NUMBER XI.

Here *Adam*, in the same Place as before, appears again, but in Union with Christ, which is to be referred to the Person of Jesus Christ, or of the Second *Adam* in our Humanity upon Earth; and is to show us the absolute Necessity of his Holy Incarnation, and immaculate Sacrifice for all Mankind, without which the great Work of our Regeneration and Reunion with *SOPHIA* could not have been wrought out to Perfection. In his Incarnation he brought that most significant Character, which the First *Adam* had lost, into the Humanity again, but first in his own Human Person, although it could not be visible in him from without, whilst he was upon Earth a Man like unto us in all Things, Sins excepted. And therefore He, and even He alone, was able and sufficient to go for us into Death, to kill Death in his own Death, to break in his Passage the Hook and Sting of Satan, to enter into, and through his dark Territory, to bruise the Serpent's Head, and to ascend up on high, to take possession of his Throne, whereby the Prophecy of *Micah* 2:13 was fulfilled, which Luther most significantly translated, es wird ein Durchbrecher fur ihnen herauf fahren: Arias Montanus, *Ascendit Effractor:* The Vulgate, *Pandens iter ante eos:* And the *English*, The Breaker is come up before them.

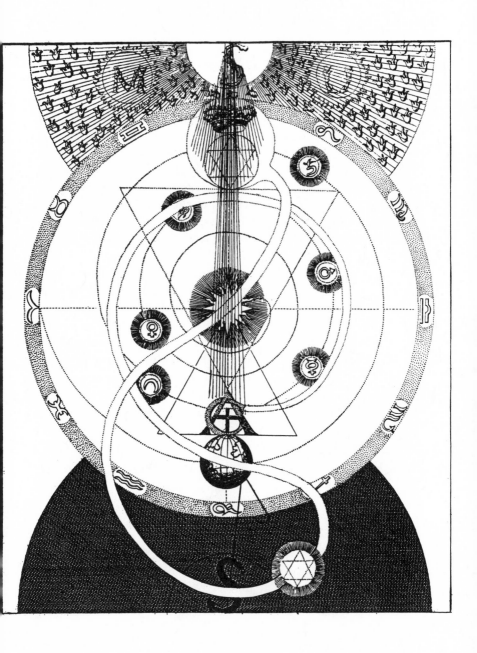

# NUMBER XII.

From the Time in which that *Breaker*, prophesied of by *Micah*, was come up before us, the Gate stood open, that the First *Adam*'s Children could follow him and enter into Paradise, which could not be done by any Soul before that Time. Holy Souls, both before and after the Deluge, that lived according to the Dictates of the Word treasured up in their Hearts, could, in their Departure from this World, go so far as to the Gate of Paradise, but Entrance could not be had by any one, till the First-Born from the Dead was entered in HIS own Person.

Yet is there still a vast Difference between Souls in their Departure from this World; and this Difference wholly depends upon the real State and Condition of that significant Character, which was spoken of before; for those Souls that have attained it in this Life to Perfection, or in other Words, those that here have put on the Heavenly Substantiality of Jesus Christ, meet with no Obstacle in their Passage. Those in whom that Character is more or less defective, meet with more or less Impediment; and those that have nothing at all of it, cannot go any further than into that Region, which most significantly is called the Triangle in Nature. O that there were none such at all!

# NUMBER XIII.

When the third Hierarchy, which *Lucifer* destroyed and de-populated, shall be completely filled again with Inhabitants from the Children of *Adam, Good* and *Evil* shall be separated, Time shall be no more, and GOD shall be All in All. This third Hierarchy, which, for good Reasons, was always hitherto represented as inferior to those of *Michael* and *Uriel*, is now here exalted again above them in the supremest Place: For as the Hierarch Jesus Christ, being the brightness of GOD the Father's Glory, and the express Image of his Person, excels all the Angels, and has by Inheritance obtained a more excellent Name than they, who are all to worship him, and to none of whom HE ever said, as HE did to him, *Sit on my Right Hand, until I make thine Enemies thy Footstool*, (Heb. 1) so also all his Subjects in this Hierarchy surpass all the Holy Angels in this, that they are Images of GOD, as manifested in all the three Principles, when the Holy Angels are only his Images, as HE was manifested in two of them: Wherefore also they are distinguished from the Angels by this peculiar Char-

acter ✡ which is not contrived by human Speculation, but is written in the Book of Nature by the Finger of God; for it points directly, not only at the Creation of this third Principle in six Days; but also at fallen and divorced *Adam*'s Reunion with the Divine Virgin *SOPHIA*.

To those who are more like (though not in their outward Shape) the Animals of this World than Men, nothing is to be said of these and the like Things, because they are Spiritual, and must be Spiritually discerned.

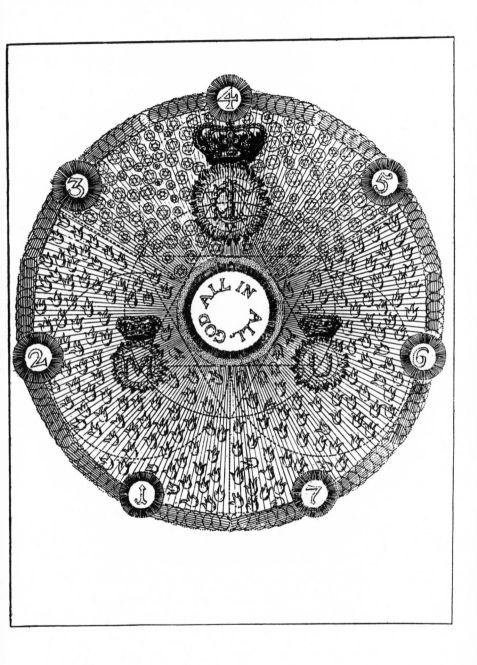

## Magnum Opus Hermetic Sourceworks

In addition to issuing the Magnum Opus Hermetic Sourceworks series, PHANES PRESS both publishes and distributes many fine books which relate to the philosophical, religious and spiritual traditions of the Western world. To obtain a copy of our current catalogue, please write:

PHANES PRESS
PO BOX 6114
GRAND RAPIDS, MI 49516
USA